What You Can DO About Media Bias

HOW TO DRAG THE MEDIA BACK TO THE MAINSTREAM

DAVID PAUL LYDAY

Three Pines Press
Kingwood, Texas, USA

Start dragging the media, pop music, television and the movies back to the mainstream today.

In this book you will find:

- Contact information for TV networks, radio, Hollywood
- Formats and suggestions for letters, emails and other communications
- Suggestions about who to go after; who to get on your side

Cover Design: Jade Design
Editor: Sylvia Cary, Cary Editorial & Book Consulting

ISBN-13: 978-0-9985756-0-5

Published in the United States of America

Three Pines Press
Kingwood, TX, USA

www.dragthemedia.com

Contents

Thank You

A few people played very important parts in the journey to this point. Some of them don't even know it. First, my wife, whose clear eye and brilliant mind helped me to see what was going on in our world. Sam Malone, the talk radio fireball behind *The Sam Malone Show*, and creator of *#corruptmedia*. Bernard Goldberg and his eye-opening book *Bias*. My friend Bob, who helped save my life. My terrific agent, Phyllis Westberg, who has been with me since the beginning.

In addition, listed in alphabetical order: Bill Bennett, Mark Davis, Larry Elder, and Hugh Hewitt, my drive-time mentors whose straight talk, strong character and dedication to the facts help make our nation stronger. Our warriors, our police and fire fighters, and all our first responders. And my friend and editor, Sylvia Cary, who did such a fine job helping get this work across the finish line.

— *David Paul Lyday*

Introduction

Is This How *You* Feel?

Do you feel that television, newspapers, radio, schools, retail stores and much of social media no longer reflect, or care about, your values, your beliefs or your wishes?

Do you have ideas shoved in your face — and in your children's faces — every day that offend you?

That you disagree with violently?

That you don't want your children exposed to?

That seem to sneer at your family and your opinions?

Do you feel as though you only get one side of the story in your daily newspaper — the "progressive" side on any controversial subject?

Does it feel to you like, overall, TV shows, movies, magazines, and popular media seem to broadcast the message that. . .

. . . Indiscriminate sex is good.

. . .monogamy and heterosexuality are non-inclusive and mean-spirited.

. . .religion provides nothing more than an endless target for late-night punch lines and ridicule in general.

. . . splatter violence in films, TV programming and video games aimed at 13-year-olds is harmless.

. . . guns in the hands of law-abiding Americans are the first step toward the next Holocaust.

Have you ever wondered why . . .

. . . stores are selling G-strings to 8-year-olds?

. . .schools are passing out birth control to sixth graders without notifying their parents?

. . .one of the choices in an action video game is braining a policeman with his own night stick?

. . . or why it is that exposing top secret intelligence operations on the front page of the world's most influential newspapers is not a crime and, in fact, will win you the newspaper industry's highest honors?

If you feel as though your viewpoint, your ideals, your lifestyle, your morals and ethics, your vision of the future, your hopes for your children and your basic idea of "truth, justice, and the American way" are being ignored and suppressed almost every day in every way, then it's time to make your opinion heard about what we allow to be peddled as "mainstream."

One other question. Does it feel as if the mainstream mainstream media's attitude is: *"You don't like it? Tough. What're you gonna do about it?"*

Well, that's what this little book is about — what you can DO about it.

Chapter 1

What is Media Bias and Why Does it Matter?

25 million people still watch
the network nightly news.

You may be thinking, "*So what?*" What's the difference if a bunch of lefty snowflakes at TV networks and *The New York Times* peddle anti-American slop? You don't watch it and you don't read it because you know it's baloney.

But here's the problem: Millions of Americans still *do* read it and watch it and listen to it. They get their information from the “mainstream media” and they believe it. They soak in the propaganda from the network news, the *New York Times, The Washington Post, The Los Angeles Times,* magazines like *Time, Newsweek* and *Vanity Fair*. Plus all the cable news networks (except, perhaps, Fox News) along with the *Huffington Post*, hip-hop radio, and social media.

When people watch “the News,” they think they're getting the *whole* story, the actual, factual data from which they can form valid opinions.

Then they **vote** based on the information they get on "the News." That's why it's critical that "the News" gives us ***all*** the information. The truth.

But the reality is, news on ABC, CBS, NBC, CNN, MSNBC, PBS, and more, leans overwhelmingly toward the progressive/leftist side on any subject. And they only give us the pieces of the news that support the leftist agenda.

Let's look at some *1984*-ish examples of left-leaning double-speak in our broadcast news:

Q. What is "mainstream" and what is "*out* of the mainstream"? Here are a few handy definitions as used by the media and Democrat elites in our government:

Ans. "*Out* of the mainstream" is anything that supports traditional American values, family values, religious values, right to life, two biological genders, traditional marriage, strong national defense, American exceptionalism, and conservative speech on college campuses. "Mainstream" is none of the above. It is anything that supports or promotes "progressive left" policies and projects.

Q. Do you know what "attacking the protection of women's health" is?

Ans. That's passing a law the makes it illegal to kill a a viable baby and sell its body parts for profit.

Q. Do you know what "the News" means when they talk about the "Muslim ban that's completely against the principles that America was founded on?"

Ans. That's taking extra time to do background checks on Middle Eastern males attempting to enter the United States from actively terrorist-controlled countries — conducting a few extra steps to make sure they're not terrorists posing as poor victimized refugees, so they can come into our country and kill Americans.

Q. How about "violating the basic constitutionally-guaranteed rights of transgendered persons."

Q. How about "violating the basic constitutionally-guaranteed rights of transgendered persons."

That's when a sovereign state — North Carolina, say — passes a law that says the federal government does not have the power to require that any male who claims to feel "confused" about his sexual identity is legally allowed to follow our wives, mothers, daughters and granddaughters into a public rest room. Yes, this has actually happened: The Obama administration attempted, by Executive Order, to require that every public facility in every state has to allow people to use the bathroom of the gender they "felt" themselves to be, rather than the gender that nature had assigned to them.

The voters of the state of North Carolina voted and passed a law that people had to use the public bathroom according to the gender *listed on their birth certificate*. They basically said, "That's an issue to be decided by the people in our state, not by the federal government."

"The News" went into orbit.

The problem as the people in North Carolina saw it was this: *Is the guy who says he's "confused" actually one of the tiny fraction of one percent of males who truly is confused — or is he a sex criminal?*

The executive order from former President *("I've Got a Phone and a Pen")* Obama did not allow for that distinction. If the male lurking by the door says he's "confused," he is allowed by government decree to follow America's women into public ladies' rooms at Target and you roll the dice.

How come the news missed that part of the discussion? discussion? All "the News" talked about was that it was "the civil rights issue of this generation." They never mentioned the men who were caught in women's bathrooms at Target taking pictures.

"The News" has power, so it is critical that it be honest and tell the whole story. But it doesn't tell the whole story. And that is wrong.

The overwhelming proportion of the half-truths, spin and non-truths the American people have been given — everything we know—everything we think, or *think* we know—about President Trump, terrorism, pro-life vs. pro-abortion, illegal immigration, Hillary Clinton's possible violation of the Espionage Act, or the economic "recovery"—comes from the mainstream media.

What We Don't Know *Can* Hurt Us

What we believe is the result of the information we are given. It is also the result of the information we are *not* given.

Exhibit One — the Benghazi Cover-Up: On September 11, 2012, The American consulate in Benghazi, Libya, was attacked by Islamist mobs. Ambassador Christopher Stevens, diplomatic officer Sean Smith, and ex-Navy SEALs Tyrone Woods and Glen Doherty, who were working as private security and intelligence contractors, were murdered in the attack.

"The News" reported it as "spontaneous demonstrations of anger over a video that had been posted to *YouTube* which devout Muslims considered blasphemous."

The problem with that story was — it was a lie.

The mobs that attacked the consulate and killed the Americans were anything but "spontaneous." They were heavily armed militia, equipped with military-grade rocket-propelled grenade launchers and heavy automatic weapons.

"The News" side-stepped all of that, stuck to the story that the murders were really just reaction to the “blasphemous video” that had simply escalated with tragic unforeseen consequences — then moved on.

The mainstream media avoided mentioning the emails showing that the State Department and the White House knew, in real time, that the attack was a military operation, and that the ambassador and other consulate personnel were in imminent danger.

The media avoided the question of what the Commander-in-Chief Obama was doing while the American ambassador to Libya was being murdered.

The media did not find it newsworthy that a series of emails showed that the White House staff and State Department staff doctored the report from the CIA — which identified the attack as a military operation — until the report had been sanitized into a bland series of talking points that supported the false narrative released by Secretary of State Hillary Clinton, and repeated on the Sunday morning news shows five times by then-UN Ambassador Susan Rice: "(A) demonstration against a blasphemous video that unfortunately took a tragic turn." The mainstream media *did,* however, cover the arrest of the maker of the supposed "inflammatory" video.

Speaking of the alleged inflammatory video — there was a tiny problem with the timeline that was also classified as *non-news* by "The News." The video had been on *YouTube* for months, and had not apparently caused any kind of "spontaneous outrage" — until the 11th anniversary of the 9/11 attacks on the World Trade Center and the Pentagon. Look up "spontaneous" in the dictionary, and it does not mention anything about waiting for months until a historically important anniversary to suddenly become outraged. "The News" missed that little detail.

Four Americans were murdered by an Islamist mob. The reason given for the atrocity was a lie. But the mainstream media didn't ask Barack Obama, who was running for re-election at the time, any questions about this lie, nor did they press Hillary Clinton, who repeated the lie — even when she stood face-to-face with the families of the dead Americans.

"The News" conducted a cover-up to help Obama's re- election campaign.

Exhibit Two — Gosnell Abortion Trial Cover-Up vs. Wendy-Mania: In the summer of 2013, the national media were entranced by the actions of a little-known Texas state senator named Wendy Davis.

State Senator Davis staged a 13-hour filibuster against a bill that would have prohibited abortion after twenty weeks of pregnancy.

At the same time, while Ms. Davis talked and talked and talked, a large pro-abortion crowd in the gallery made so much noise, it was impossible for the Texas legislature to conduct business. The raucous Wendy-maniacs gummed up the works so completely that the midnight deadline for voting on the bill was missed.

The media scooped the story up and Wendy Davis became front page news overnight—*The Washington Post, New York Times,* CBS, ABC, NPR, CNN, MSNBC, *Huffington Post, Time, USA Today*.

At around the same time as Wendy Davis' pro-late-term-abortion filibuster was going on, so was the horrifying trial of Kermit Gosnell.

The Philadelphia abortionist was charged with killing seven viable babies by slicing their spinal cords.

Gosnell was indicted for killing the newborns, and also for the deaths of two women who had come to his filthy abortion clinic and had died on the table.

The Gosnell murder trial lasted for more than 50 days, and, according to Media Research Center, never once made "The News." It seems inconceivable that for fifty-six consecutive days the network news ignored the trial of a man accused of murdering seven babies and being responsible for the death of two women. When the verdict came down and Gosnell was found guilty, it made one small blip on the network TV screen, then disappeared again.

The eight-week trial of one of America's most brutal abortionists didn't make a ripple, yet one State Senator's diatribe against increasing controls on aborting viable babies was national news.

Is it possible that the hideous details of the Gosnell case were suppressed in the mainstream media because the whole gruesome business might reflect badly on the abortion-on-demand industry?

Who Decides What Is and Isn't "News?

The networks have daily meetings during which they decide what's "news" and what's "not news."

The 13-hour rant against any restrictions on late-term abortion — legislation designed to prevent a repeat of Gosnell's atrocities — was "big news." A man on trial for brutally killing seven living babies was "not news."

The media could have covered both sides; the two stories were clearly related. They chose only to cover one side.

If the news media don't bother to mention. . .

- the dereliction of duty in the Obama administration over the murder of four Americans in Benghazi and the subsequent cover-up;
- the destruction of thousands of official emails in the investigation of subversion of the IRS;
- the deaths of DEA agents in the "Fast and Furious" weapons debacle;
- the military veterans who are dying while waiting for treatment in the VA medical system;
- the fact that 17,000 scientists call "global warming/climate change" a bogus concept;
- the possibility that because of Hillary Clinton's private email server, America's enemies may have known everything we planned to do in international actions before we did it;

- the numerous illegal aliens who are committing rapes and murders in American cities,
- or even that fact that the Obama White House was in the loop as members of the FBI actively worked to try to help Hillary Clinton beat Donald Trump in the 2016 election. . .

. . . then you have absolutely no way of knowing the whole story.

That is what we need to fix!

Chapter 2

"Why Doesn't Somebody Do Something?"

If the media won't come to the mainstream,

we'll take the mainstream to the media.

If the mainstream media continues to ignore or tear down the values you cherish and are trying to pass on to your kids, and if you feel what's being reported daily may even be harmful to this country — then it's time for somebody to do something about it.

You are that "somebody" and this book gives you very specific suggestions on exactly what you can do to take the fight right to the media even though they don't think anyone can touch them. Boy, have we got a surprise for them! Here's how it's going to work:

- We'll tell you what scares them
- We'll tell you how to talk to them about what's upsetting you
- We'll suggest what to use for leverage
- And we'll tell you *who* to talk to.

Ready. . . Set. . . Change the World!

How would you like to see the mainstream media give the pro-life side of the abortion argument right next to a headline such as, "GOP Attempts to Slash Funding to Planned Parenthood"?

How about seeing the media involved in as relentless an investigation into what happened in Benghazi, or Hillary Clinton sending classified emails over her non-secure homebrew server ... as they have been in the Mueller investigation into alleged “collusion” between the Trump campaign and “the Russians”?

Imagine how you’d feel if the newspapers and TV and magazines all presented a balanced view of the "human-caused global warming" question, rather than treating the huge group of reputable scientists who *don’t* agree like a bunch of Holocaust deniers?

How can you start making those goals a reality? Here’s a hint.

Follow the money. If you want to pressure a money-making entity into changing something they are doing, threaten their money supply. Often just letting them know that you can take away enough of their income to hurt does the trick.

You can blog, you can blow up social media, you can email, you can phone.

You can take advantage of the websites supporting traditional values and ideas, such as Tim Wildmon's American Family Association website, www.afa.com, www.OneMillionMoms.org or Brent Bozell's Media Research Center, all of which provide links for petitions, and also for letters to the management of selected companies and organizations. You can sign the letters electronically and send as-is or edit for yourself.

Or you can do it the old-fashioned way: Write an actual letter, put it in an envelope, address it to the Chairman's office and fire it off.

If you want to regain some control over the institutions that were supposedly created to serve *you* ... but no longer do so . . then *follow the money.*

Figure out where their income flows from; then use your preferred channel to tell them you are unhappy and why; and finally, suggest that if they are not going to do something to make you less unhappy, you are going to take some of that cash flow away.

Next steps: So if you don't like what's happening your network news or on your cable news or on your local news coverage, then take a crack at them. Use one or more of the weapons listed above: Blog, tweet, call, email or write a letter. To help you do this, contact lists are provided at the end of this book and in most cases you can get updates on these contacts by checking out the company's website. Think how good you'll feel . . .now that you know you have the power to actually help fix the problem.

Chapter 3

The Rules

Before you jump in, here are a couple of simple rules to keep in mind. These rules apply to every medium, every venue, and every action that I talk about in this book.

Start at the top. Send a letter (or email) to the CEO, the president, the chairman, the man or woman whose name is on the sides of the company's trucks. Tell them why you're upset. If it's about a particular story, let them have it with both barrels. Be as specific as possible. If it's more general (the slanted-one-way-or-the-other issue), tell them that you will no longer watch their news coverage if they don't become un-slanted. And make sure they know that you will be in contact with the companies that advertise on the news broadcasts.

Get a name and make sure it's the right one: Always start your letter "Dear Mr. Everett," rather than "Dear Sir," or "To Whom it May Concern." It's more powerful, you look more businesslike, and it means something different.

Think about yourself. If you are the owner of Smith's Sporting Goods, don't you feel differently about "Dear Ms. Smith" than you do "Dear Owner?"

Think globally. Complain locally: You certainly want to make your outrage known to the network top brass, but the people who feel it most when you say "I will no longer watch your station" are the management at the local affiliate. They're the ones whose commercials become less easy to sell when the ratings on their broadcasts of network shows in their own town start to sag.

It will take a few extra minutes to look up addresses, but with today's technology, sending out your letter to half a dozen different people only takes five extra minutes, and it's worth every one of them.

Contact the advertisers: These are the people who are spending their money to put their commercials on the program that you are no longer going to watch.

Send your criticism to several people: In the case of the TV networks, in addition to the president of the network, you'll also want to send one to the VP of sales, the head of programming or the president of the news division, and the general manager of the local network affiliate in your town. They say "all politics is local." That is certainly true in this case as well

The real news here is that, to borrow the famous quote from the movie *Network,* if you are mad as hell, you don't have to take it anymore.

Chapter 4

How to Talk to Your Television

Step-by step instructions for taking the fight

to the networks, including sample letters

Let's get specific.

Say you want to write a letter to a TV network to tell them you are unhappy because of something they've put on the air.

Maybe you are upset about a network story you consider a typical example of what President Donald Trump calls "fake news." Since that term has now almost become a household word, you can let them know you can spot a "fake news" story a mile away, and they are guilty! So you might write:

September 24, 20xx

Mr. Joseph Jones
President FYI Television Network
1000 Uptown Avenue
New York, NY 10000

Dear Mr. Jones:

I was outraged by a story on your network news program last Thursday night. During the news,

President Trump was repeatedly called a racist, but your reporters never asked the accusers for their evidence. [Or] *You ran a story that claimed ______________, but I know for a fact that _______________ is not the whole story. (Then give additional facts, or tell how you feel about their distortions, or relate any other relevant circumstances you feel must be considered to get the whole picture).*

I guarantee I will not watch the news on your network again until you are willing to give both sides of the story. The news is supposed to give us the real facts, not somebody's agenda.

In addition to writing you, I will be contacting the sponsors of your nightly news show to tell them I won't be watching your news, and why.

Regards,
(Your Name)

Cc: Oscar Woofer, Woofer's Dog Food
Max Mertz, Breath Bomb Mouthwash

You're welcome to use any or all of the language in this sample if you like, however use *your own words* as much as possible. You can write a better letter about how you feel than anybody else can. Your personal take on something makes for a much more authentic-sounding letter.

Be specific. Get the facts right. "Wrong" facts will derail your mission. We win when we combine correct facts with our personal reaction to something. That's what changes minds and gets action.

You can send the same letter to the network's Vice President of news and Vice President of sales. Just get those names right.

Letters to locals

Here's a sample letter to the network affiliate in your town. You are basically using the same letter you'd send to the bigwigs, although you may want to change some details to make it more effective for a local station.

Ms. Mary Marvel
Station Manager
KFYI TV
My Town, IA

Dear Ms. Marvel:

I was outraged by a story on your network news program last Thursday night. During the news, President Trump was repeatedly called a racist, but your reporters never asked the accusers for their evidence. [Or] You ran a story that claimed _______________, but I know for a face that ________________ is not the whole story. (Then give additional facts, or tell how you felt about their distortions, or relate any other relevant circumstances you feel must be considered to get the whole picture).

I guarantee I will not watch the news on your station again until FYI Network is willing to give both sides of the story. The news is supposed to give us the real facts, not somebody's agenda.

In addition to writing you, I will be contacting the local sponsors of your nightly news show to tell them I won't be watching your news, and why.

Regards,
(Your Name)

Cc: Ms. Penny Posh, President
Swanky Stores

I recently sent two identical letters of complaint ... one to the network division president at a major network and the other to the general manager of that network's affiliate in my town.

I did not receive any response from the network division president, but I got a reply instantly from the general manager at the local station. His letter was polite, somewhat apologetic, and asking for a little slack.

Local stations that are losing local viewers and local revenue because of decisions made by somebody in midtown Manhattan are in a tough spot. They are suffering damage for something they have almost no control over.

But you can be quite sure that a general manager of a local station who gets too many letters is going to let the suits "up there" know about it.

Secondary Boycott

Definition: A group's refusal to work for, purchase from, or handle the products of a business with which the group has no dispute.

If you think networks and local TV stations hate to "get letters," let's talk about advertisers — sponsors. They're paying anywhere between thousands and hundreds of thousands of dollars for thirty seconds to try to sell their product to the audience. If you want to talk to somebody who *really* doesn't want to hear that you are going to stop watching a particular program, put your mouth where their money is.

Warning: Do not threaten the advertiser that you will stop buying the product because the company is sponsoring the offending show. Inform the company that is spending its money to buy advertising time on the show that you will no longer watch the show (at least until it makes some changes) and why.

Known as a “secondary boycott,” it is actually against the law to boycott someone because of something they have no control over. However, while the advertiser does not control the content of the program, they can sure make their feelings known if they are starting to get less bang for their buck because of choices made by the people who do control the content.

OneMillionMoms.com does an excellent job walking this line. Through their omm@afasv.net emails, they will send requests to those on their distribution list such as “Urge Kroger to No Longer Sponsor ‘American Housewife.’”

In the accompanying email, they will specify their reasons for objecting to the particular show, and provide a letter to the advertiser which can be signed by you.

When you write to an advertiser, the same rules mentioned above also apply. *Start at the top*. Send a letter to the president or the CEO. Some CEOs will throw letters away. But some take it very personally if they get a letter containing the thought that “your company should be ashamed to be associated with. . .” If the company is named after someone’s family — if there is a real Jack Sprat sitting in the CEO’s office at Jack Sprat Weight Loss Clinics — that’s the name you address with the first letter. Then you hit the director of marketing, the director of sales, and the advertising manager.

The ad manager is the person who has probably made the recommendation about the show in question. But they will happily switch horses if there's a problem.

Unless a television show is a runaway hit, TV shows are something of a commodity. You can reach just about as many people in your target audience with the 19th-rated show as you can with the 17th-rated show. And if nobody is writing letters about number 19 with threats to stop watching the show, it's a pretty easy choice.

Oscar Woofer, Chairman
Woofer's Dog Food
101 Dalmatian Street
Dogwood, Tennessee

Dear Mr. Woofer:

I was outraged by something I saw last Thursday night on the news broadcast that you sponsor. During the news, President Trump was repeatedly called a racist, but the network's reporters never asked the accusers for their evidence. [Or] They ran a story that claimed so-and-so, but I know for a fact that so-and-so is not the whole story. (Give your own facts, or tell how you feel about their distortions).

I admire your product and your company. But I guarantee I will not watch the news on FYI until they are willing to give both sides of the story.

Regards,
(Your Name)

cc: Director of Marketing
Advertising Manager

Don't Just Sign Off . . . Sound Off

Let's take a moment to summarize. If you stop watching programming or news on a network as a protest, don't do it quietly.

The networks say. "If they (the complainers) don't like it, they can turn the TV off," which is true, but it doesn't have the impact that you want.

When you let them, and their all-important sponsors, know that you are boycotting their show, station or network, you multiply your effectiveness.

I Heard it on *The Sam Malone Show*

This idea sprang to life one evening during rush hour while I was listening to talk radio fireball Sam Malone. Sam is the creator of ***#corruptmedia.*** It's the Twitter version of a barroom brawl.

Sam's subject of controversy that particular night was not the usual politics, it was advertising. Specifically, it was the decision by a national beer brand to sign a well-known "gangsta" rapper as part of their marketing effort.

The question Sam was asking his radio audience was whether they approved. Of course some people called in to say they thought the choice was cool, and that the beer maker had every right to hire a performer who appealed to young-ish males, who are certainly a primary demographic for beer. But there were also a number of people who called in to say they were upset by the choice of performer by the brand. The comment came up over and over again that "Somebody ought to *do* something."

A call finally came in to the show with a suggestion for "something" that people could do. "Vote with your dollars."

Sam quickly agreed, "Absolutely, I have many times times stopped buying a product if I didn't like something they were doing."

As I was nodding along with Sam and the caller, it hit me, right there in the traffic, that "Vote with your dollars" was only half the answer. The whole answer was, *"Vote with your dollars—and then tell them about it."*

The fact is, the five or ten or twenty dollar-per-week drop in sales when I stop, or you stop, or Sam stops buying something isn't much of a blip on the radar of a multi-billion dollar brand.

But if you let the advertiser *know about it*, you've scored a bulls-eye.

Let me mention one more time, because this is where it all started: If you like to use social media to make your views known, you will have a blast at *#corruptmedia*. Get in there and mix it up. Also, check Sam Malone out at *sammalone.com* and at *facebook.com/pages/Sam-Malone-Show*.

It's time to give the mainstream media and the leftist conspiracy something they're not used to. Americans who fight back.

So. . .

Step one, stop buying.

Step two, tell them you're stopping and why.

Step three, wait for results.

If you just stop watching, they lose one TV household out of a hundred thousand, or 20 million. It makes you feel better, but it does nothing to cause the network to change anything.

Multiply your anger for a thousand

On the other hand, if you write and tell them and their sponsors that you have stopped watching the show because (fill in the thing you didn't like), they start multiplying by a thousand in their heads.

Sponsors and broadcasters figure every angry letter they get represent *a thousand people* who think the same way, but didn't take the time to write a letter, find a stamp and mail it.

By the time they've gotten a letter from you, a letter from the friend you coerced into writing, and half a dozen more from people who heard you talk about it on the radio, using the "times-a-thousand" factor, they're starting to look at some significant losses.

Losing audience—and ultimately advertising dollars—is the one thing even the oldest, boldest, glossiest network ultimately cannot accept.

When you got 'em by the eyeballs, their hearts and minds will follow:

Here's why regular people—at least, a large number of regular television-watching people like you and me—can shiver a worldwide media superpower. *Without us, they're out of business.*

Television is an *Audience Delivery Medium.*

Television likes to be thought of as an entertainment medium, a cultural medium, a news medium, a reasoned political discourse medium, an educational medium.

Maybe.

Bottom line, television is *an audience delivery medium.* That is its business.

The biggest networks in the business survive *only* long as they can get a big enough audience to attract money from sponsors.

The most powerful communications entities in the world can be convinced to change if the alternative to changing is the loss of the one thing they can't do business without — their audience.

How to Find Contact Information for TV

In Chapter 7, you can find information about how, and who, to contact at both broadcast and cable TV networks.

You can get even more details using the website information in chapter 7 and searching individual websites for the network you want to contact. Click "About Us," and you will usually be able to find a link to a list of officers. *(Source: www.parentstv.org, updated 2018)*

To find contact information for *local* television stations, also go online and look under the call letters of the station, or go to the online version of your local newspaper. You may have to click on "Entertainment," then "Television," then "Contact" where you then may have a choice of "Networks" and "Local stations."

You can find contact information for major daily and local newspapers by looking in the papers themselves, by searching online by the name of the paper, or going on the organization's or company's website.

One thing you know for sure about entities that are in the business of selling commercial time is that they make it pretty easy for people to contact them.

The person looking for contact information might be an irate viewer like you, but you also might be a local plumbing contractor with four locations and a hundred thousand dollars to spend on local TV advertising.

The stations in your town want to be found.

Chapter 5

Television: Don't Just Change the Channel. Change the Shows!

"All that is necessary for the triumph of evil is that good men do nothing."

– Edmund Burke, English philosopher

Okay. We all know they slant the TV news.

And we are beginning to open our eyes to the fact that they also slant the TV *shows*.

In fact, OneMillionMoms.com and the American Family Association (www.afa.net) both broke the news that the Disney Channel will broadcast a show that includes two small boys kissing each other on the lips.

OneMillionMoms.com also took aim at Fox's new hit, "The Mick." In one episode, two 13-year-old boys are sitting naked in a bathtub waiting for an older girl to get back with some drinks so they can have a threesome. Welcome to "family-friendly viewing."

A lot of today's TV programs are pro-abortion, pro-drug, pro- a lot of things that we don't want 7-year-olds exposed to. But there they are, spewing cultural sewage into our living rooms at 8:00 every night.

Children See . . . Children Do?

Why does it matter what's on television?

Because our kids see it. Their friends see it. Television gets talked about at school, in lunchrooms, online, across social media.

Sure, you can turn it off—but it would still be there in millions of homes, leaking toxic waste into middle school minds.

Can You Do Anything About It? Yep.

The good news is — you don't have to "take it or leave it," the way the networks would like to treat your outrage for what they're showing your kids. You can help change the things you and your kids see on TV

And maybe the difference we can make is not just a difference in the quality of the programming the big networks think they can shove down the throats of the typical American family.

Maybe it's a difference in the future direction of the country. Here's what you can do.

Step One: Just Say No

First, take control of television in your house. Use the "Parental Controls" tools. And if all else fails, no television in the kids' rooms. If your kids are watching things you don't want them to watch, you're partly at fault.

Step Two: Start Dragging Network TV to the Mainstream

Take dead aim on the people who are shoveling stuff you find unacceptable into your living room:

Write a letter to the network.

Send a copy of the same letter to your local network station. The local General Manager feels pressure from a lot smaller hit, and has local merchants to think about.

Watch the show you want to drag back to the mainstream—just enough to find out who the current sponsors are.

Write the sponsors a letter. (NOTE: When OneMillionMoms asked people to do something about "The Mick," the owner of *MyPillow* pulled his advertising from the show.)

Check out the sample letter below; this can help you get started.

Sample Letter

Use the prototype letters we offer here, but edit or change where appropriate. Also send a copy to the local network affiliate.

Dana Walden and Gary Newman
Co-Presidents, Fox Entertainment
Fox Broadcasting Co.
10201 W. Pico Blvd.
Los Angeles, CA 90035

Dear Ms. Walden and Mr. Newman:

The recent episode of ("Name of show") was appalling. (Tell what happened on the show.) Is that really the message you want to give to your audience. Especially an audience that's largely made up of tweens and teens?

The next time there's a news story about a 13-year-old having sex with a teacher, we'll remember you ran this episode.

Also, you can bet that I will contact your sponsors, and let them know that I will not watch this dreadful show they are spending their money to sponsor, until Fox changes the content. This is "cultural pollution." It must make you very proud.

Regards,
(Your Name)

Kick Their Ads

You do not have to suffer in silence.

In order to change things, you first have to make sure the networks know how mad you are, and that they get your message in a way that makes it as hard as possible for them to ignore you.

Here's what you do. As discussed, blog, tweet, call, Email or write a letter.

But the important thing to remember is to *be specific* as to what program you are referring, what offended you about it, and how you feel about what you saw. The less generic you can be, the more effective you will be. If you write the president of the TV network a letter that says, "I hate you," you are less likely to get what you want than if you write, "I will no longer watch your shows because all of them are filled with (fill in specifics about what you are no longer willing to watch)."

You can send the same letter to the network's senior vice president of programming and vice president of sales if you like.

The sales VP is the person whose yearly bonus depends on getting sponsors for all the network's shows.

The head of programming knows that his or her boss, the network president, has gotten a copy of the letter, and, for him or her, that's bad. The job in programming is to select and develop shows that will get the network more viewers and drive up the price of 30-second commercial slots. If letters start coming in from people who hate the new shows, the head of programming with a high-six figure income and the nifty lifestyle in Manhattan will be the traffic manager at a station in Tierra del Fuego.

Chapter 6

How to Stop the Presses from Spinning

Get rid of "fake news" and news "spin," or Americans will do it for you.

Ever since Donald Trump beat Hillary Clinton in the 2016 election, newspapers have given up even pretending to give unbiased reporting of the news.

Just the facts, ma'am? Not so far.

The mainstream media has declared war on the President of the United States with an almost bizarre level of hysteria. They've printed false, vicious stories about him and his family. And when their stories turn out to be lies, they shrug and say, "Hey, we just printed it. We didn't say it was true."

The non-existent Trump "dossier." Global warming. Crimes committed by illegal aliens. Sanctuary cities. What is the newspaper in your town talking about? Is it fair and balanced on these issues? Most likely not.

The *New York Times*, the *Washington Post, USA Today,* all lead with anti-Trump, anti-conservative, anti-traditional American values, without batting an eye. Stories that offer facts in support of the opposite side are often missing.

Stop the Presses!

Newspapers need advertisers.

Simple.

The same rules apply as for taking the fight to the biggest TV networks in the world.

Follow the money.

If we want the newspapers to change the way they distort the news: 1) stop reading the paper; and 2) make sure we let their advertisers know we are no longer reading the paper–so we're no longer seeing the ads they are paying to run in the paper.

NOTE: To get the most bang for your buck, look through the paper and see who buys to most space–the paper's biggest advertisers. Those are the businesses you send letter to first.

Let's take a shot:

C.R. Banner
Publisher

The Daily Banner
Dear Mr. Banner:

I am a long-time reader of the Banner. But I can no longer tolerate the paper telling only half of every story.

If the paper does not adopt a policy of presenting both sides of controversial subjects, I will cancel my subscription, and I will also contact your major advertisers to let them know that I am canceling my subscription, and why. (NOTE: Pick your own subjects here: *"If you present news stories about_______, then also cover the_______.")*

If you talk about "global warming," also talk about (studies that contradict the idea, negative effects on jobs, the death of the American coal industry—your call). I am simply asking that you present ALL the news.

I will wait two months. If the paper hasn't committed to change its approach, I will take the promised action, and I will encourage others to do the same.

Regards,
(Your Name)

Cc: Editor in Chief
Advertising Sales Manager

Send an advance letter to the target advertisers if you feel like it.

IMPORTANT: You are not threatening to boycott the advertiser. You are merely informing them that they may soon be losing ad impressions for which they are paying lots of money to the newspaper.

Ready for another sample letter?

Ms. Penny Posh, President
Swanky Stores
Houston, Texas

Dear Ms. Posh:

As one of the major advertisers in the Banner, *you should be aware that I have informed them I will cancel my subscription if they do not take steps to make their news coverage more fair and balanced.*

As I wrote to Mr. Banner, I am not asking the paper to suppress news, nor to slant it. I am simply asking that the paper present both sides of controversial issues.

I have given them two months to show response to the request. If there has been no change at that time, I will cancel the Banner *and ask as many of my acquaintances as possible to do likewise.*

Regards,
(Your Name)

Cc: Advertising Manager

The point here is that you don't necessarily want to destroy the daily newspaper. It might be nice to continue to get the paper you've been getting for decades with sports, funnies, ads for your favorite stores and BOTH SIDES OF THE STORY. If it turns out that they would rather maintain an agenda than respond to their readers, then you take them down.

Tactical considerations

You don't want to write a hundred letters, so make tactical choices, as the advertisers do, and the way they do it in a political campaign.

Start with the big advertisers. Count which advertiser has the most pages and be aware of the size of the ads for a week.

Give priority to local advertisers. A big local store is more likely to feel the loss of eyeballs than a global cell phone company.

Localize it even more if you feel it gives you better leverage. A business in your ZIP code that spends a lot of money in the paper is going to be more sensitive to the loss of you as a reader than the loss of somebody 50 miles west of town.

Pick businesses of which you are a customer, or a potential customer. At the risk of being politically incorrect, a letter from a male to a hardware store might have a little more juice than from the same male to a nail salon.

"Welcome to Network News — and on Tonight's Agenda We Have . . ."

There is one other, darker possibility — that it's not unintentional. If the information is being suppressed in the service of an agenda, rather than simply passed over by otherwise well-meaning journalists, that is a *really* big story.

Chapter 7

Drag Them Screaming and Kicking — & CONTACT LISTS

Got a problem with stores peddling trash to our kids? Hollywood "values?" Music lyrics? Disgusting ads?

In spite of the fact that media bias is finally getting some press of its own, and even though we are getting better at spotting agenda-driven situations, it's all still flourishing, sometimes in unexpected situations.

Toy Story

Have you recently gone clothes shopping for a daughter or niece at a local store and taken a look at the styles for pre-teen and tween girls? G-strings for 8-year-olds? And in the toy store, violent or sex-themed video games? Does it makes you feel like blowing your stack?

If you would like to give these stores notice that they will lose your business if they don't stock more modest clothing choices for young girls, or produce less violent and brutal "first person" video games for your elementary school kids, here's a **contact list** for some of the major national dry goods and electronics stores, video game manufacturers and major clothing companies.

CONTACT LIST for DRY GOODS & ELECTRONICS STORES, VIDEO GAME MANUFACTURES & CLOTHING COMPANIES

Wal-Mart, Inc.
Wal-Mart Stores, Inc.
Doug McMillon, President and CEO
Bentonville, AR 72716-8611
Tony Rogers, Executive Vice President
Chief Marketing Officer
www.walmart.com

Sears
Sears
Edward Lampert, President & CEO
3333 Beverly Road
Hoffman Estates, IL 60179
847-286-2500
www.sears.com

Target
Target
Brian Cornell, CEO
1000 Nicollet Mall
Minneapolis, MN 55403
Rick Gomez
EVP, Chief Marketing Officer
Dustee Tucker Jenkins
SVP, Chief Communications Officer
www.target.com

Costco
Jeffrey Brotman, Chairman of the Board
W. Craig Jelinek
President and CEO
Corporate Office
999 Lake Drive
Issaquah, WA 98027
www.costco.com

JCPenney
JCPenney Company, Inc.
6501 Legacy Drive
Plano, TX 75024
(972) 431-1000
Marvin R. Ellison
Chairman and CEO
Mary Elizabeth Stone West
EVP, Chief Marketing Officer
Joseph McFarland
EVP, JCPenney Stores

Best Buy
Hubert Joly, Chairman and CEO
Mike Mohan, Chief Marketing Officer
Best Buy
Corporate Headquarters
7601 Penn Ave S, Minneapolis, MN 55423
612-291-1000
https://corporate.bestbuy.com/about-best-buy

Macy's
Macy's Inc.
7 W Seventh St
Cincinnati, OH 45202

Phone Number: (513) 579-7000
Fax Number: (302) 636-5454
Website: http://www.macys.com
Email: Website: http://www.macys.com
Executives
Jeff Gennette, President and CEO
Richard Lennox, Chief Marketing Officer
https://www.macysinc.com/about-us

Nordstrom
Nordstrom, Inc.
1617 Sixth Avenue
Seattle, WA 98101-1707
Phone (206) 628-22111
Fax Number: (206) 628-1795
Website:
http://www.nordstrom.com
Executives
CEO: Blake W. Nordstrom
CFO: Michael G. Koppel
COO: Erik B. Nordstrom

Gap
The Gap, Inc.
2 Folsom St
San Francisco, CA 94105
Phone Number: (415) 427-0100
Fax Number: (415) 427-0275
Website: http://www.gapinc.com

Executives
Jeff Kirwan, President and CEO, The Gap
Sonia Syngal, President and CEO, Old Navy
TJX

TJ Maxx, Marshall's, Home Goods
East Campus
The TJX Companies, Inc.
770 Cochituate Road
Framingham, MA 01701
Main Number: 508-390-1000
West Campus
The TJX Companies, Inc.
300-400 Value Way
Marlborough, MA 01752
Main Number: 508-390-1000

Kohl's
Kohl's Department Stores
N56 W17000 Ridgewood Drive
Menomonee Falls, WI 53051
Phone: (262) 703-7000
www.kohlscorporation.com

Can't Find Movies for Families and Kids?

If you can't find movies that are suitable for your family, you have several choices:

1) you can stay home;

2) you can vote with your dollars and only go to see movies that meet with your personal approval;

3) you can let theater owners know how much money they are losing by showing the offensive, violent, overly sexualized junk that Hollywood insists on.

It seems as though Hollywood *does* have a liberal agenda, but most likely the only agenda theater owners have is making enough money to stay open and pay back the huge amounts Hollywood demands from theaters in the first place. Let the theater chains know directly that you would attend their theaters more if they had different movies to show. Let them take that up with the movie makers.

CONTACT LIST FOR SOME MAJOR THEATRE CHAINS

AMC Theatres - Official site of AMC Theatres, the international movie theater chain. Featuring showtimes, online ticket sales, theater finder, and information on the latest movies.
www.amctheatres.com

Regal Entertainment Group (NYSE:RGC) - Operates a nationwide theatre circuit comprised of Regal Cinemas, United Artists Theatres, and Edwards Theatres.
www.regalcinemas.com

Cinemark Theatres - Official site of Cinemark Theatres, a major motion picture exhibitor which recently acquired Century Theatres, with screens throughout North America.
www.cinemark.com

Landmark Theatres - Nationwide theatre circuit that shows independent films, foreign language cinema,

restored classics, and documentaries. Includes polls, list of theatres with showtimes and features from their own publication FLM Magazine.
www.landmarktheatres.com

Carmike Cinemas - Motion picture exhibitor with screens in small and mid-sized communities across the United States.
www.carmike.com

Kerasotes Theatres, Inc. - Independent chain in the Midwest with theatres across Illinois, Indiana, Missouri, Ohio, and Iowa.
www.kerasotes.com

National Amusements, Inc. - Owner of the Showcase Cinemas and many other theatres throughout the United States, the United Kingdom, and Latin America.
www.nationalamusements.com

Marcus Theatres (NYSE:MCS) - Operates nearly 500 screens in Wisconsin, Illinois, Ohio, and Minnesota.
www.marcustheatres.com

Mann Theatres - Owns and operates theatres in California and Colorado. *www.manntheatres.com*

Harkins Theatres - With locations throughout Arizona.
www.harkinstheatres.com

Muvico - Operates megaplex theaters in entertainment centers.
www.muvico.com

Loews Cineplex
Find movie showtimes, trailers, local theaters, and purchase movie tickets for Loews Cineplex and AMC Theatre locations.
www.loewscineplex.com

Clearview Cinemas - Movie theatres located throughout the New York metropolitan area. Site provides theatre locations and show times, information on currently playing movies, gift certificates, and more. A Cablevision company.
www.clearviewcinemas.com

Cinema Grill - Relax, dine, and simultaneously see a movie.
www.cinemagrill.com

Seen Any Offensive TV Commercial Lately?

We all see TV spots we don't like. Fifty percent of TV spots graduated in the bottom half of their class. That's not what this is about. This is about a TV commercial you see with a message that you think is harmful. If you see a commercial that you think glamorizes cruelty or greed or immorality, let the advertisers know you're upset. You can act through a number of organizations such as Onemillionmoms.com or American Family Association or the Family Research Council. Or you can contact the company directly.

Since there are literally thousands of advertisers, rather than list contact information, we provide a general blueprint for finding your particular advertiser's information. As a demonstration, we'll use the world's largest retailer, Procter and Gamble.

CONTACT LIST FOR SOME MAJOR ADVERTISERS ON TV:

Procter & Gamble

On the P&G landing page, click on "Our Brands" at the top of the page, and you will find a list of advertisers to contact such as: Always, Bounty, Charmin, Crest, Dawn, Downy, Febreze, Gillette, Head and Shoulders, Herbal Essence, Luvs, Olay, Old Spice, Oral B, Pampers, Swiffer, Tampax, Tide, Vicks and many others.

Once you are on the home page of the brand, find "Contact" or "Contact Us" at the top or bottom of the home page. Click on that. You should find an 800 number, an email link, and possibly a mailing address. Also links for social media.

Website for US operations: http://us.pg.com/

CONTACT LIST for ORGANIZATIONS TO HELP YOU GET NEEDED INFORMATIONS

American Family Association: www.afa.net
The American Family Association monitors media, films, publication, etc., for material and messages it considers objectionable by traditional standards, and serves as a channel for protest in such situations.

One Million Moms: www.onemillionmoms.com
In their own words, "OneMillionMoms.com was begun to give moms an impact with the decision-makers and let them know we are upset with the messages they are sending our children and the values (or lack of them) they are pushing."

Family Research Council: www.frc.org
Quoting from the website: "Family Research Council's vision is a culture in which human life is valued, families flourish and religious liberty thrives."

Media Research Center: www.mrc.org
Brent Bozell's MRC relentlessly monitors media bias in all channels, in all things said, and all things suppressed, and provides the conservative public with tools for response.

Parents Television Council: www.parentstv.org
The mission of the PTC is to protect children and families from graphic sex, violence and profanity in the media, because of their proven long-term harmful effects. Our vision is to provide a safe and sound entertainment media environment for children and families across America.

CONTACT LIST FOR TELEVISION NETWORKS

ABC
77 W. 66th St.
New York, NY 10023
(212) 456-7777
www.abc.com

ABC Entertainment
2040 Avenue of the Stars
Los Angeles, CA 90067
(310) 557-7777
www.abc.com
E-Mail: netaudr@abc.com
Anne Sweeney, Co-Chair,
Disney Media Networks
President, Disney/ABC Television Group

NBC
30 Rockefeller Plaza
New York, NY - 10112
(212) 664-4444
www.nbc.com
Steve Burke, CEO
NBC Universal
Andrew Lack, Chairman
NBC News

NBC Entertainment
5750 Wilshire Blvd
Los Angeles, CA 90036
(818) 840-4444
Bonnie Hammer, Chairman
Cable Entertainment Group

Email: nbcshows@nbc.com
http://www.nbcuniversal.com/

CBS
51 W. 52nd Street
New York, NY 10019-6188
(212) 975-4321
www.cbs.com/feedback
Joseph Ianiello, President and
Chief Executive Officer

CBS Entertainment
7800 Beverly Blvd
Los Angeles, CA 90039-2112
(323) 575-2747
www.cbs.com
Glenn Geller
President, CBS Entertainment
Chris Ender
Executive Vice President, Communications
CBS Corp.
(818) 655-1100
cender@cbs.com

Fox Broadcasting Co.
10201 W. Pico Blvd.
Los Angeles, CA 90035
(310) 369-1000
E-Mail: askfox@foxinc.com
Dana Walden and Gary Newman
Co-Presidents

John F. Swope, President
Public Broadcasting Service (PBS)
1320 Braddock Pl.
Alexandria, VA 22314
(703) 739-5000
www.pbs.org

John Ford, President, Programming
Ion Media Networks
601 Clearwater Park Road
West Palm Beach, FL 33401
(561) 659-4122
http://www.ionline.tv/

Telemundo
2290 W. Eighth St.
Hialeah, FL 33010
(305) 884-8200
www.telemundo.com

Univision
605 Third St.
New York, NY 10158
(212) 455-5200
www.univision.com

Mark Pedowitz, President
CW Network
3300 Olive Ave.
Burbank, CA 91505
(818) 977-2500
www.cwtv.com

CONTACT LIST for CABLE NETWORKS

ABC Family Channel
Paul Lee, President
3800 West Alameda Ave.
Burbank, CA 91505
(818) 560-1000
Fax: (818) 560-1930
http://freeform.go.com/

A&E Television Networks
235 East 45th Street
New York, NY 10017
(212) 210-1340
fax: (212) 850-9304
www.aande.com
Email: aefeedback@aenetworks.com

AMC
200 Jericho Quadrangle
Jericho, NY 11753
(516) 803-4360
www.amctv.com

A&E Television Networks (History Channel)
235 E. 45th St.
New York, NY 10017
(212) 210-1400
www.aande.com

BET
1 BET Plaza
1900 W. Street, NE

Washington, DC 20018
(202) 608-4BET
www.bet.com

Bravo
c/o NBC Entertainment
3000 W. Alameda Avenue
Burbank, CA 90036
www.bravotv.com

Cartoon Network
Cartoon Network
1050 Techwood Drive
Atlanta, GA 30318
(404) 885-2263
www.cartoonnetwork.com

CNN
1 CNN Center
Atlanta, GA 30348
(404) 827-1700
Fax: (404) 827-1099
www.cnn.com/feedback

Comedy Central
1775 Broadway
New York, NY 10019
(212) 767-8600
www.comedycentral.com

Court TV
Viewer Comments
600 Third Avenue

New York, NY 10016
(800) COURT-56
www.courttv.com

Discovery Communications, LLC
John S. Hendricks
Chairman
1 Discovery Place
Silver Spring, MD 20910
(240) 662-2000
Fax (240) 662-1868
http://corporate.discovery.com

The Disney Channel
3800 W. Alameda Ave.
Burbank, CA 91505
(818) 569-7500
http://disneychannel.disney.com/

E! Entertainment TV
5750 Wilshire Boulevard
Los Angeles, CA 90036
(323) 954-2400
www.eonline.com

ESPN / ESPN2
ESPN Plaza
935 Middle Street
Bristol, CT 06010
(860) 585-2236
www.espn.com

Fuse
700 N Central Ave, Fl 6
Glendale, CA 91203
(323) 543-2762
www.fuse.tv

FX
P.O. BOX 900
Beverly Hills, CA 90213-0900
www.fxnetworks.com

Game Show Network, LLC
Jen Minezaki
Director of Public Relations
2150 Colorado Ave. Ste. 100
Santa Monica, CA 90404
(310) 255-6933
Fax (310) 255-6810
http://www.gsn.com
jminezaki@gsn.com

Hallmark Channel
12700 Ventura Blvd.
Suite 200
Studio City, CA
(888) 390-7474
http://www.hallmarkchannel.com/

Home Box Office (HBO)
1100 Avenue of the Americas
New York, NY 10036-6737
(212) 512-1000
www.hbo.com

Lifetime Television
309 W. 49th Street
New York, NY 10019
(212) 424-7293
www.lifetimetv.com

MTV Networks
c/o MTV Studios
1515 Broadway
New York, New York 10036
www.mtv.com

Nickelodeon
Viewer Services
1633 Broadway
New York, NY 10019
(212) 258-7579
www.nick.com
www.nick-at-nite.com

Oxygen
75 Ninth Avenue
New York, NY 10011
www.oxygen.com

Sci-Fi Channel
8800 W. Sunset Blvd., 4th Floor
West Hollywood, CA 90069
(310) 360-2300
www.syfy.com

Showtime Networks
1633 Broadway

New York, NY 10019
(212) 708-1600
www.showtimeonline.com

TBS
1 CNN Center
P.O. Box 105366
Atlanta, GA 30348-5366
(404) 827-1700
www.turner.com
Email: tbsinfo@turner.com

TLC (Owned by Discovery Communications, LLC)
John S. Hendricks
Chairman
1 Discovery Place
Silver Springs, MD 20910
(240) 662-2000
Fax: (240) 662-1868
www.corporate.discovery.com

TNT
1010 Techwood Drive
Atlanta, GA 30318
(404) 885-4538
email: tnt@turner.com
www.tnt.com

USA Networks
1230 Avenue of the Americas
New York, NY 10020
(212) 413-5000

VH1
1515 Broadway
New York, New York 10036
(212) 258-6000
www.vh1.com
(Source: www.parentstv.org, retrieved March, 2017)

Radio Broadcasters: Always remember that radio stations — like every other advertising-dependent entity we're discussing—are not in the business of spreading filth. They're in the business of making money. If they can make money spreading positive messages, they will do that. And if it is going to hurt the bottom line to push songs about beating up women and killing police officers, and shouting racial slurs for America's children to repeat, they will probably stop.

CONTACT LIST FOR RADIO NETWORKS

iHeartRadio Network
www.iheartradio.com

ABC Radio Networks
Martha Luszcz, (212) 735-1718
New York, NY 10022

American Public Media
Joe Eskola, (651) 290-1058
480 Cedar Street
Saint Paul, MN 55101

American Urban Radio Networks
Glenn Bryant (412) 456-4040
960 Penn Avenue
Pittsburgh, Pennsylvania 15222
E.J. Williams, (212) 297-2571
432 Park Avenue South, 14th Floor
New York, New York 10016

The Associated Press
Thom Callahan, (202) 736-1105
1825 K Street, N.W.
Washington, DC 20006-1253

Bloomberg L.P.
Chris Brown, (212) 617-3224
731 Lexington Avenue
New York, NY 10022

Crystal Media
Nick Krawczyk (703) 247-7500
1100 Wilson Boulevard, Suite 800
Arlington, VA 22209
Pam Foster, (212) 922-1601
60 East 42nd Street, Suite 5250
New York, NY 10165

Dial-Global Communications
David Landau, (212) 967-2888
Charles Steinhauer, (212) 967-2888
220 West 42nd Street, 28th Floor
New York, NY 10036

Google
Scott Bogdan, (949) 791-1200

680 Newport Center Drive, Suite 150
Newport Beach, CA 92660

Jones MediaAmerica, Inc.
Susan Garone, (212) 556-9428
Cathy Csukas, (212) 556-9439
1133 Avenue of the Americas, 11th Floor
New York, NY 10036

Latino Broadcasting Company
Gustavo Pombo, (305) 857-6660
1133 Avenue of the Americas, 11th Floor
New York, NY 10036

National Public Radio
Jackie Nixon, (202) 513-2818
Lori Kaplan, (202) 513-2000
635 Massachusetts Avenue, NW
Washington, DC 20001

Premiere Radio Networks
Len Klatt, (818) 461-5119
15260 Ventura Blvd., 12th Floor
Sherman Oaks, CA 91403

Public Radio International
Michael Arnold, (610) 892-7300
Craig S. Oliver, (301) 593-9880
100 North Sixth Street- 900A
Minneapolis, MN 55101

Radio Research Consortium
Joanne Church, (301) 774-6686
Carl Nelson, (301) 774-6686

18200 Hillcrest Avenue
Olney, MD 20832

Reach Media
Marla H. Bane, (972) 789-1058
13760 Noel Road, Suite 750
Dallas, TX 75240

Salem Radio Network
Tom Tradup, (972) 831-1920
6400 North Beltline Road, Suite 210
Irving, TX 75063

Sporting News Radio Network
Clancy Woods, (847) 400-3033
1935 Techny Rd, Suite 18
Northbrook, IL 60062

Stratus Media
Glenn Felty, (212) 808-4641
494 8th Avenue, 16th Floor
New York, NY 10001

Traffic.com
Diana Desimone, (610) 407-7431
851 Duportail Road
Wayne, PA 10087

Susan Moore
(212) 869-1111
James M. Higgins
(212) 869-1111
25 West 45th Street
New York, NY 10036-4902

Univision Radio
Jack Hobbs, (214) 525-7737
3102 Oaklawn Avenue, Suite 215
Dallas, TX 75219
Kathleen Bohan (212) 310-6053
477 Madison Avenue New York, NY 10022

USA Radio Networks
Tim Maddoux, (972) 484-3900
2990 Springlake Road, Suite 107
Dallas, TX 75234

Wall Street Journal Radio Network
Paul Bell, (212) 597-5606
1155 Avenue of the Americas, 8th Floor
New York, NY 10036

Westwood One Radio Networks
Paul Bronstein, (212) 641-2024
40 West 57th Street (5th Floor)
New York, NY 10019

WOR Radio Networks
Paul Siebold, (212) 642-4558
111 Broadway, 3rd Floor
New York, NY 10006
(Source: Arbitron web site)

CONTACT LIST FOR SOME MAJOR NATIONAL NEWSPAPERS

USA Today
JOANNE LIPMAN

Editor-in-Chief
7950 Jones Branch Drive
McLean, VA 22108
(703) 854-3400
www.usatoday.com
Craig Kaplan
VP, Advertising Sales
New York Office
ckaplan@usatoday.com

The New York Times
Dean Baquet
Executive Editor
620 8th Ave
New York, NY 10018-1618
(212) 556-7777
www.nytimes.com
Senior Vice President, Advertising
Lisa Howard
(212) 556-7809
lisa.howard@nytimes.com

The Wall Street Journal
Gerard Baker
Editor-in-Chief
1211 Avenue of the Americas
New York, NY 10036-8701
(800) 568-7625
www.wsj.com

Los Angeles Times
Chris Argentieri
Sr. Vice President and General Manager202 W. 1st St.
Los Angeles, CA 90012

(213) 237-5000
www.latimes.com

New York Post
Michelle Gotthelf
Metro Editor
1211 Avenue of the Americas
New York, NY 10036-8790
(212) 930-8500
www.nypost.com

The Washington Post
Cameron Barr
Managing Editor
1150 15th St. NW
Washington, DC 20071
(202) 334-6000
www.washingtonpost.com

Chapter 8

And Then There is Washington

As I was proofing this book before publication, I had *Fox News* on TV in the background – *Hannity*. He was talking about the forces working against President Trump and second on his list was ***the media***. The show's host Sean Hannity stressed the importance of not just sitting back, but "fighting back." One of his guests, former conservative presidential candidate Herman Cain, mentioned a White House "comment hotline" you can call between 9 a.m. and 4 p.m. (ET) to leave the President a "we've got your back" kind of message: **(202) 456-1111.**

That might be a good place to start. Let your first action in your personal campaign to ***Drag the Media Back to the Mainstream*** be a supportive message to our President because we've all got to pitch in and DO something. So I repeat:

Who cares what the "mainstream media" is up to?

We care.

We *have* to care.

About the Author

David Paul Lyday

David Paul Lyday is a veteran ad agency executive, award-winning copywriter, and creative director. He has seen, from the inside, how the mainstream media work. With his unique perspective, he provides everyday Americans with information they may never have had before—how to make the "mainstream media" listen to them. Lyday is also a published novelist and a screenwriter.

Three Pines Press
Houston, Texas, USA
www.dragthemedia.com

www.ingramcontent.com/pod-product-compliance
Lightning Source LLC
Chambersburg PA
CBHW050557280326
41933CB00011B/1876

* 9 7 8 0 9 9 8 5 7 5 6 0 5 *